LEGO® NEXO KNIGHTS™

BUILD YOUR OWN ADVENTURE

CONTENTS

MEET ROBIN

This is Robin Underwood. He loves to build! When he is not studying at the Knights' Academy, he is dreaming up new gadgets and gear for the knights and putting them together in his high-tech workshop. He may not be one of the knights just yet, but the rest of the team would be lost without him.

Robin's plume is made from feathers

Merlok 2.0 appears as a hologram

TECHNICAL WIZARDRY

Robin works closely with Merlok 2.0 – the computer operating system who used to be a flesh-and-blood wizard. Merlok's magic and wisdom are at the heart of the knights' technology. Let's hope nothing bad happens to him!

A sturdy helmet protects Robin in battle

Crossed spanners are a symbol of Robin's skill with machinery

1

2

Robin is young, so he is not as tall as the knights

ROBIN'S BATTLE SUIT

Robin designed this brilliant Battle Suit himself. When he's at the controls, he is ready to face any danger that threatens the Kingdom of Knighton. The suit has a rapid-fire six-shooter cannon, a huge shield for self-defence, and long, powerful legs for covering great distances. But most importantly of all, it has Robin's quick-thinking brain!

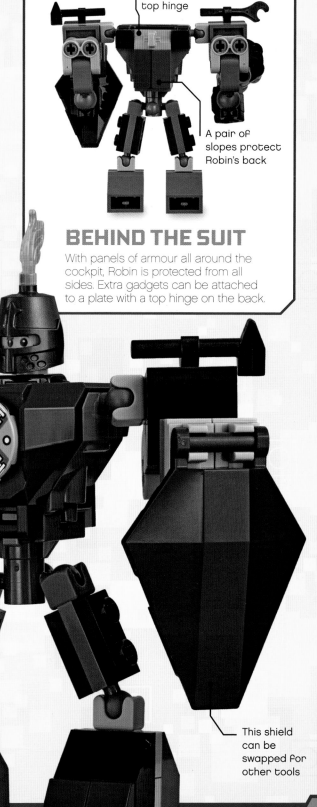

REAR VIEW

2x2 plate with top hinge

A pair of slopes protect Robin's back

BEHIND THE SUIT

With panels of armour all around the cockpit, Robin is protected from all sides. Extra gadgets can be attached to a plate with a top hinge on the back.

The suit has its own built-in tool kit!

Turn this cog to fire the stud shooter

WHO ARE YOU CALLING A JUNIOR KNIGHT?

Ball joints allow the legs and arms to move in all directions

This shield can be swapped for other tools

MODEL INSTRUCTIONS

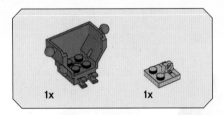

1x   1x

1

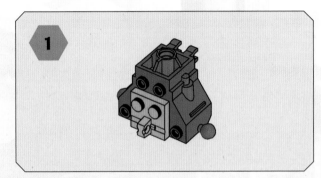

1x   2x

2

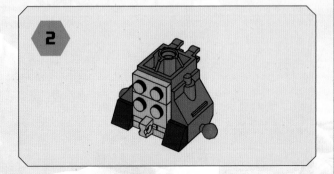

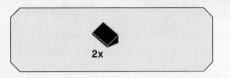

2x

3

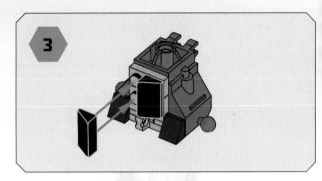

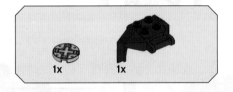

1x   1x

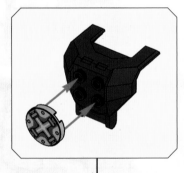

4

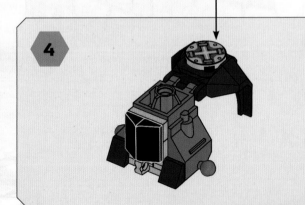

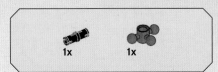

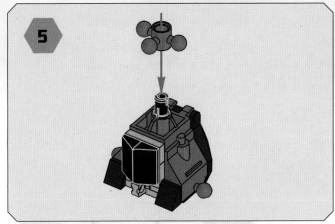

5

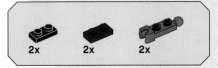

1 **2**

2x

FOLLOW THE INSTRUCTIONS CAREFULLY!

6

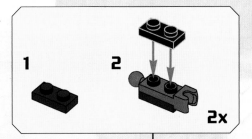

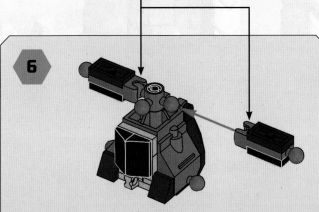

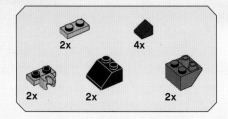

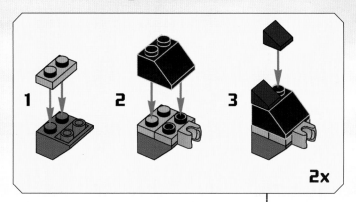

2x

7

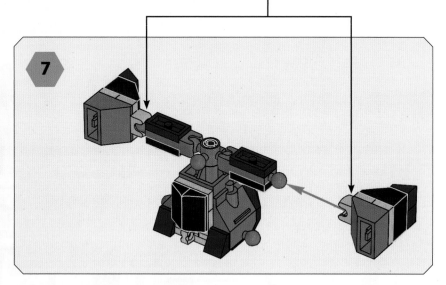

8

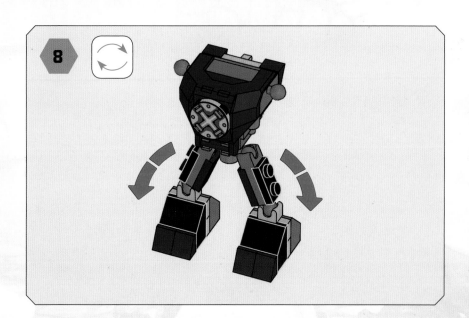

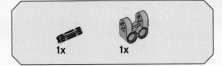

1x   1x

9

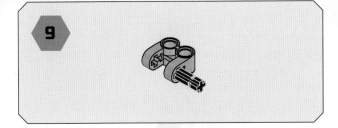

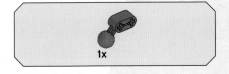

1x

10

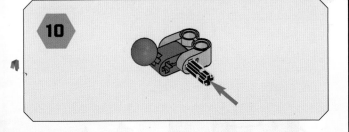

1x

11

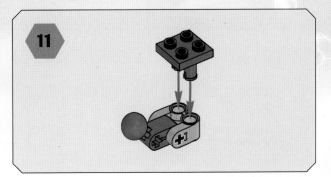

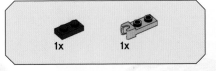

1x   1x

12

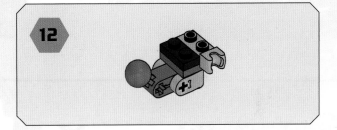

1x

13

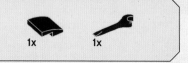

1x   1x

14

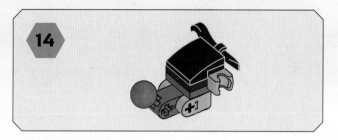

1x

15

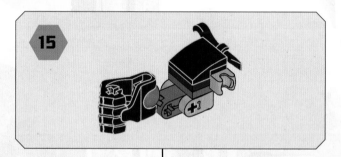

16

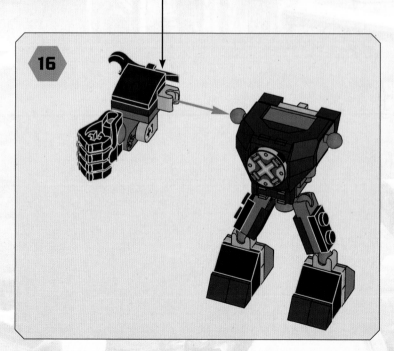

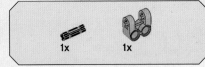

1x   1x

17

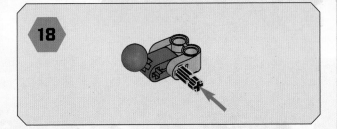

1x

18

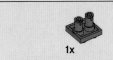
1x

19
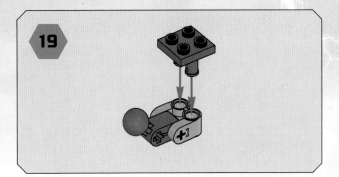

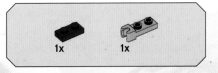

1x   1x

20
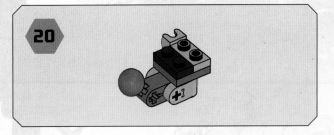

1x

21
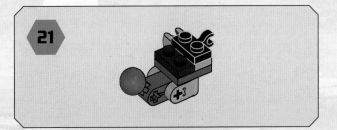

22

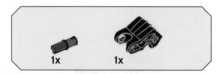

23

24

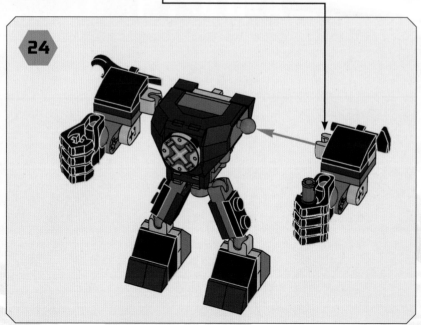

1x   1x

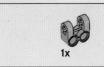

1x

25

CLICK

咔嗒

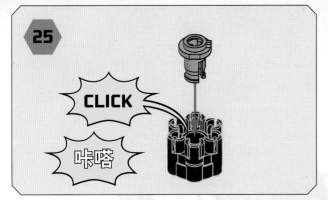

27

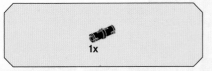

1x

1x

28

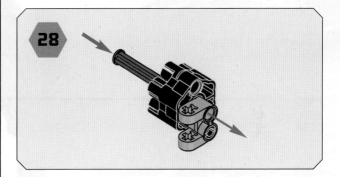

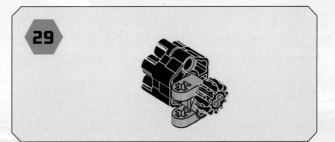

1x

26

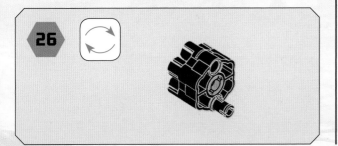

29

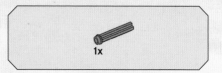

1x

30

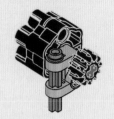

31

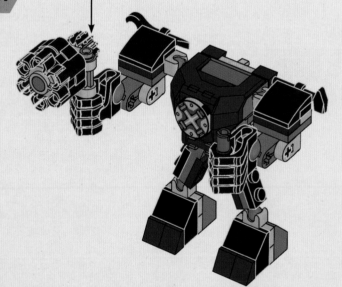

ALMOST THERE!

1x

32

2x

33

1x

34

35

36

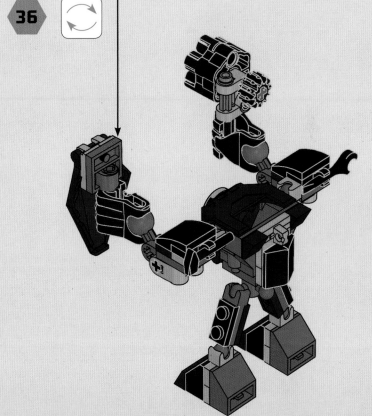

12x

37

38

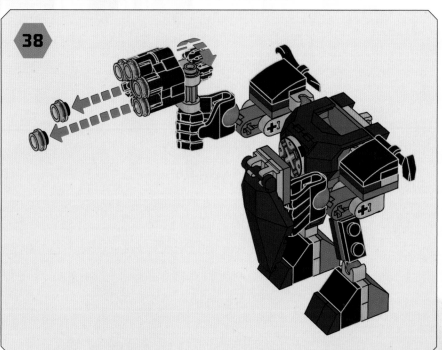

39

40

BUILD YOUR OWN ADVENTURE

In the pages of this book, you will discover an exciting LEGO® NEXO KNIGHTS™ adventure story. You will also see some clever ideas for LEGO NEXO KNIGHTS models that might inspire you to create your own. Building LEGO models from your imagination is creative and endlessly fun. There are no limits to what you can build. This is your adventure, so jump right in and get building!

HOW TO USE THIS BOOK

This book will not show you how to build the models, because you may not have exactly the same bricks in your LEGO collection. It will show you some useful build tips and model breakdowns that will help you when it comes to building your own models. Here's how the pages work...

Breakdowns of models feature useful build tips

"What will you build?" flashes give you even more ideas for models you could make

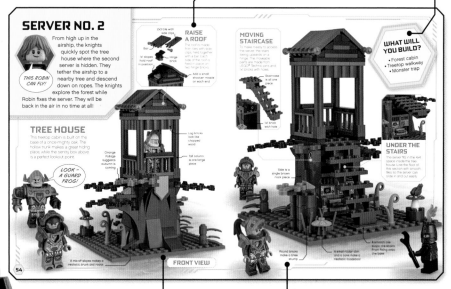

SERVER NO. 2

From high up in the airship, the knights quickly spot the tree house where the second server is hidden. They tether the airship to a nearby tree and descend down on ropes. The knights explore the forest while Robin fixes the server. They will be back in the air in no time at all!

THIS ROBIN CAN FLY!

RAISE A ROOF

The roof is made from tiles with side clips, held together with a bar. Each side of the roof is fixed in place on two hinge bricks.

2x3 tile with side clips

Bar

1x1 slopes hold roof in position

Hinge brick

Add a small shooter missile on each end

MOVING STAIRCASE

To make it easy to access the server the stairs swing upwards on a hinge. The moveable parts are made from LEGO® Technic pins and 1x1 bricks with holes.

Staircase is all one piece

1x1 brick with hole

WHAT WILL YOU BUILD?

• Forest cabin
• Treetop walkway
• Monster trap

TREE HOUSE

This treetop cabin is built on the base of a once-mighty oak. The hollow trunk makes a great hiding place, while the sentry box above is a perfect lookout point.

Orange foliage suggests autumn is coming

LOOK – A GUARD FROG!

Log bricks look like chopped wood

Tall column is one large piece

UNDER THE STAIRS

The server fits in the 4x4 space inside the tree house. Line the floor of this section with smooth tiles so the server can slide in and out easily.

Side is a single brown rock piece

A mix of slopes makes a realistic trunk and roots

FRONT VIEW

Round bricks make a tree stump

A small radar dish and a cone make a realistic toadstool

A smooth tile slope tile slopes up from Riding onto the base

LET'S GET GOING!

Sometimes, different views of the same model are shown

Special features or elements on models are annotated

HELLO, I'M JASON BRISCOE.

MEET THE BUILDER

Jason Briscoe is a LEGO fan and super-builder, and he made the inspirational LEGO models that can be found in this book. To make the models just right for the LEGO NEXO KNIGHTS world, Jason worked with the LEGO NEXO KNIGHTS team at the LEGO Group headquarters in Billund, Denmark. Use Jason's models to inspire your own amazing builds.

BEFORE YOU BEGIN

Here are five handy hints to keep in mind every time you get out your bricks and prepare to build.

Organise your bricks
Save time by organising your bricks into colours and types before you start building.

Be creative
If you don't have the perfect piece, find a creative solution! Look for a different piece that can create a similar effect.

Research
Look up pictures of what you want to build online or in books to inspire your ideas.

Have fun
Don't worry if your model goes wrong. Turn it into something else or start again. The fun is in the building!

BUILD ME AN ARMY – IF YOU DARE!

Make your model stable
Make a model that's sturdy enough to play with. You'll find useful tips for making a stable model in this book.

TILE

When you want a smooth finish to your build, you need to use a tile. Printed tiles add extra detail to your models.

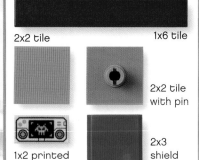

2x2 tile

1x6 tile

2x2 tile with pin

1x2 printed tile

2x3 shield tile

BUILDER TALK

Did you know that LEGO® builders have their own language? You will find the terms below used a lot in this book. Here's what they all mean:

STUD

Round raised bumps on top of bricks and plates are called studs. A chain has a single stud at each end. Studs fit into "tubes", which are on the bottom of bricks and plates.

2x2 corner plate

Chain

MEASUREMENTS

Builders describe the size of LEGO pieces according to the number of studs on them. If a brick has 2 studs across and 4 up, it's a 2x4 brick. If a piece is tall, it has a third number that is its height in standard bricks.

1x1 brick

1x2 brick

2x2 brick

2x4 brick

1x1x5 brick

HOLE

Bricks and plates with holes are very useful. They will hold bars or LEGO Technic pins or connectors.

1x1 brick with hole

2x3 curved plate with hole

2x2 round brick

1x2 brick with two holes

4x4 round brick

CLIP

Some pieces have clips on them, into which you can fit other elements. Pieces such as ladders fasten onto bars using built-in clips.

1x1 plate with vertical clip

1x1 plate with horizontal clip

2x3 tile with clips

SIDEWAYS BUILDING

Sometimes you need to build in two directions. That's when you need bricks or plates like these, with studs on more than one side.

1x4 brick with side studs

1x1 brick with two side studs

1x2/2x2 angle plate

1x1 brick with one side stud

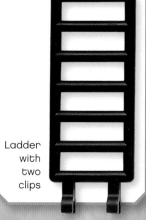

Ladder with two clips

BRICK

Where would a builder be without the brick? It's the basis of most models and comes in a huge variety of shapes and sizes.

 2x2 brick

 1x2 brick

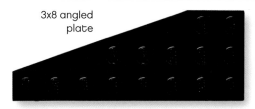 1x2 textured brick

 1x1 headlight brick

 1x2 grooved brick

 2x2 domed brick

1x1 round brick

PLATE

Like bricks, plates have studs on top and tubes on the bottom. A plate is thinner than a brick – the height of three plates is equal to one standard brick.

 3x8 angled plate

1x8 plate with side rail

 2x3 plate

1x2 jumper plate

 2x2 round plate

 1x1 tooth plate

 1x1 round plate

 1x2 plate with top ring

 4x4 curved plate

 4x4 round plate

SPECIAL PIECES

Special pieces are used to create specific structures, or to link the build to a LEGO theme.

 1x1 pyramid

 4x4 rocky angled slope

 4x4 angled slope

2x2 angled corner tile

 2x2 rocky plate

1x5x4 inverted half arch

 4x4 printed radar dish

SLOPE

Slopes are bigger at the bottom than on top. Inverted slopes are the same, but upside down. They are smaller at the bottom and bigger on top.

1x2 slope

1x2 Inverted slope

HINGE

If you want to make a roof that opens or give a creature a tail that moves, you need a hinge. A ball joint does the same job, too.

 1x2 hinge brick and 1x2 hinge plate

Hinge plates

 1x2 hinge brick and 2x2 hinge plate

 Ball joint socket

 Hinge cylinder

 2x2 brick with ball joint

 1x2 plate with click hinge

WELCOME TO KNIGHTON

Knighton is no ordinary kingdom. Though at first glance Knighton looks almost old-fashioned, everything in it runs on high-tech digital technology. It was once a peaceful realm – but all that has changed. It's now under attack from terrifying Stone Monsters, led by an evil jester called Jestro. King and Queen Halbert are counting on the NEXO KNIGHTS™ heroes to save Knighton!

KING AND QUEEN HALBERT

Knighton's royal couple rule their kingdom justly, in good times and very bad. They are advised by Merlok 2.0, a hologram-wizard. Merlok also helps the knights by creating digital powers for them to download.

> WILL WE EVER SEE PEACE AGAIN?

JESTRO AND MONSTROX

Jestro, the king's old jester, isn't really bad – he's just easily led. Monstrox, an evil wizard in the shape of a cloud, zapped Jestro with lightning, making him evil too. With Stone Monsters under their control, this duo is dangerous!

> KNIGHTON WILL SOON BE OURS!

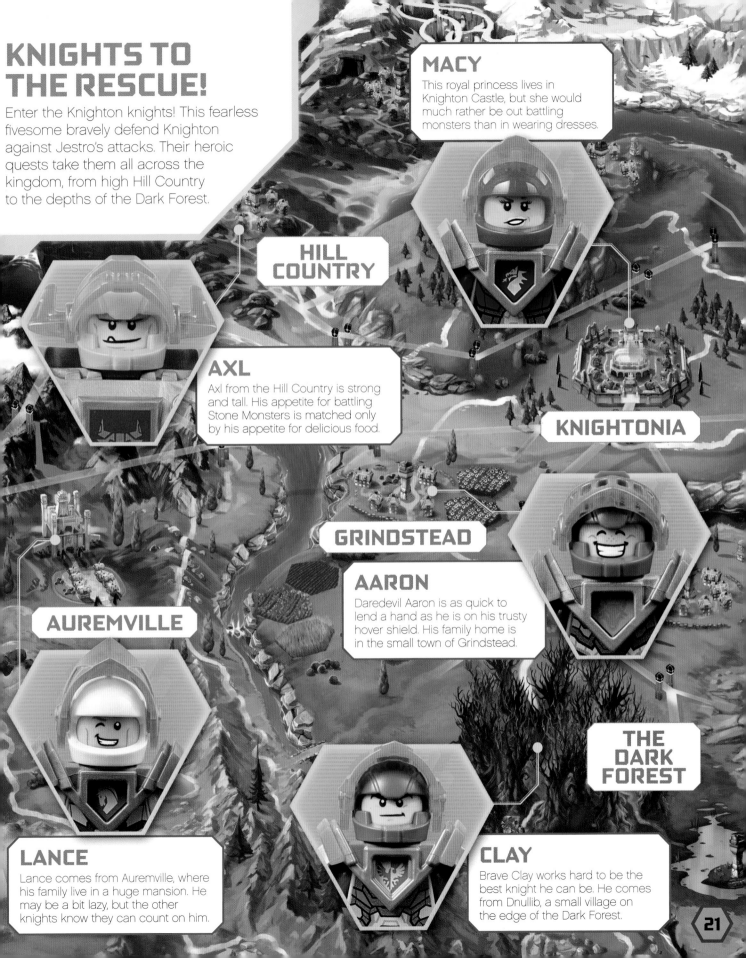

KNIGHTS TO THE RESCUE!

Enter the Knighton knights! This fearless fivesome bravely defend Knighton against Jestro's attacks. Their heroic quests take them all across the kingdom, from high Hill Country to the depths of the Dark Forest.

MACY

This royal princess lives in Knighton Castle, but she would much rather be out battling monsters than in wearing dresses.

HILL COUNTRY

AXL

Axl from the Hill Country is strong and tall. His appetite for battling Stone Monsters is matched only by his appetite for delicious food.

KNIGHTONIA

GRINDSTEAD

AARON

Daredevil Aaron is as quick to lend a hand as he is on his trusty hover shield. His family home is in the small town of Grindstead.

AUREMVILLE

THE DARK FOREST

LANCE

Lance comes from Auremville, where his family live in a huge mansion. He may be a bit lazy, but the other knights know they can count on him.

CLAY

Brave Clay works hard to be the best knight he can be. He comes from Dnullib, a small village on the edge of the Dark Forest.

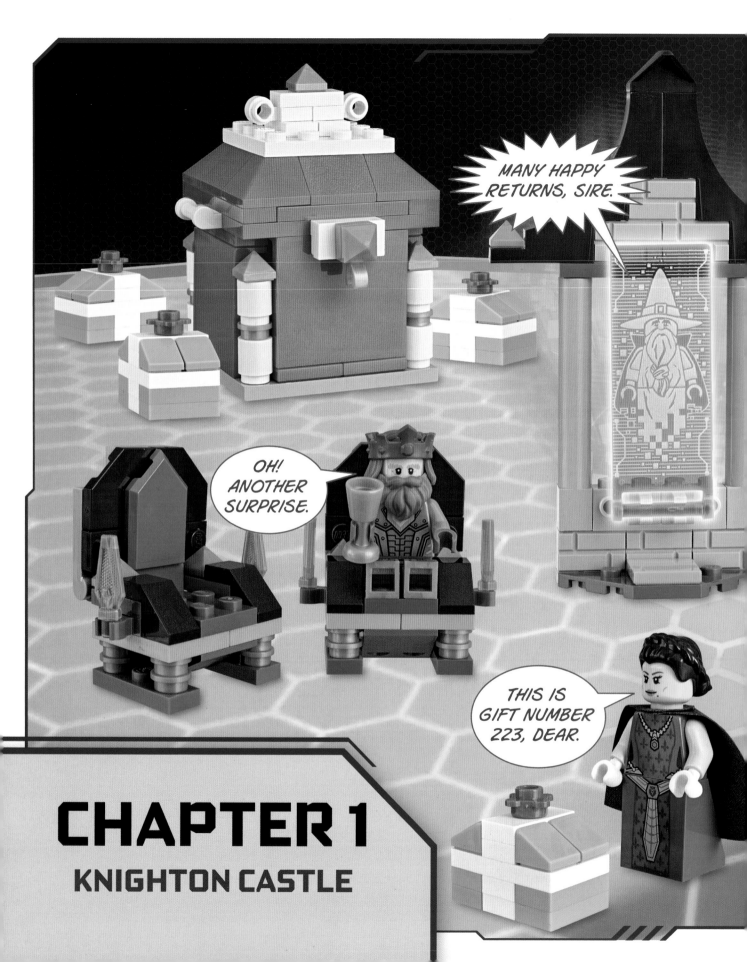

CHAPTER 1
KNIGHTON CASTLE

HOORAY FOR HALBERT!

HAPPY BIRTHDAY, DAD!

Hip-hip-hooray! It's King Halbert's birthday and everyone in Knighton is celebrating. The five knights – Clay, Aaron, Macy, Axl and Lance – are putting on a show of their skills in the Joustdome. The king and queen watch from their thrones.

BACK BASICS

Royals love to relax, so these thrones are built as recliners with tilting backs! Plates with clips and plates with bars make the simple hinge mechanism.

1x2 plate with side clip

1x2 plate with side bar

REAR VIEW

THRONES

Use gold pieces and lots of details to make a throne fit for a king or queen. As you build, make sure there is room for a minifigure to sit in it!

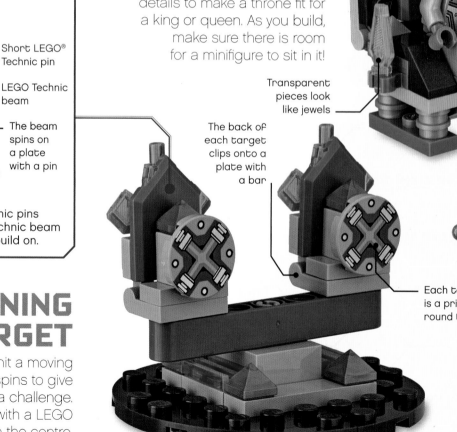

Transparent pieces look like jewels

King Halbert fits this throne perfectly

Short LEGO® Technic pin

LEGO Technic beam

The beam spins on a plate with a pin

Short LEGO Technic pins plugged in a LEGO Technic beam act as studs to build on.

The back of each target clips onto a plate with a bar

Each target is a printed round tile

SPINNING TARGET

It's hard to hit a moving target – this one spins to give the knights an extra challenge. It turns on a plate with a LEGO Technic pin in the centre.

Long LEGO Technic pin

1x1 brick with hole

Plates with rings above

The target swings on a hinge made from two long LEGO Technic pins that slot into pieces with holes.

Knights score extra points for hitting these side flags

Jumper plates hold the outer ring together

Outer ring is made from four curved bricks

TALL TARGET

This target is tall, but it doesn't tip over because it has a broad base. When a knight hits the target, it swings back and forth – and the knight scores a point!

LEGO Technic cylinder

The base is made from four curved plates

Sideways small plates wth teeth make pointy horse ears

Seat is a motorbike body

HOVER HORSE

Lance loves showing off his skills on a Hover Horse. This turbo-charged model has a powerful engine, chunky handlebars, sleek angles and lots of cooling vents for added horsepower.

Flanks are large angled slopes built sideways on angle plates

1x2 curved slope

Round plate with hole

FRONT OF THE HORSE

The horse's head is built around a piece more usually used to make robot bodies. It fits onto a plate with a clip so it can move up and down.

Robot body piece

1x2 plate with clip

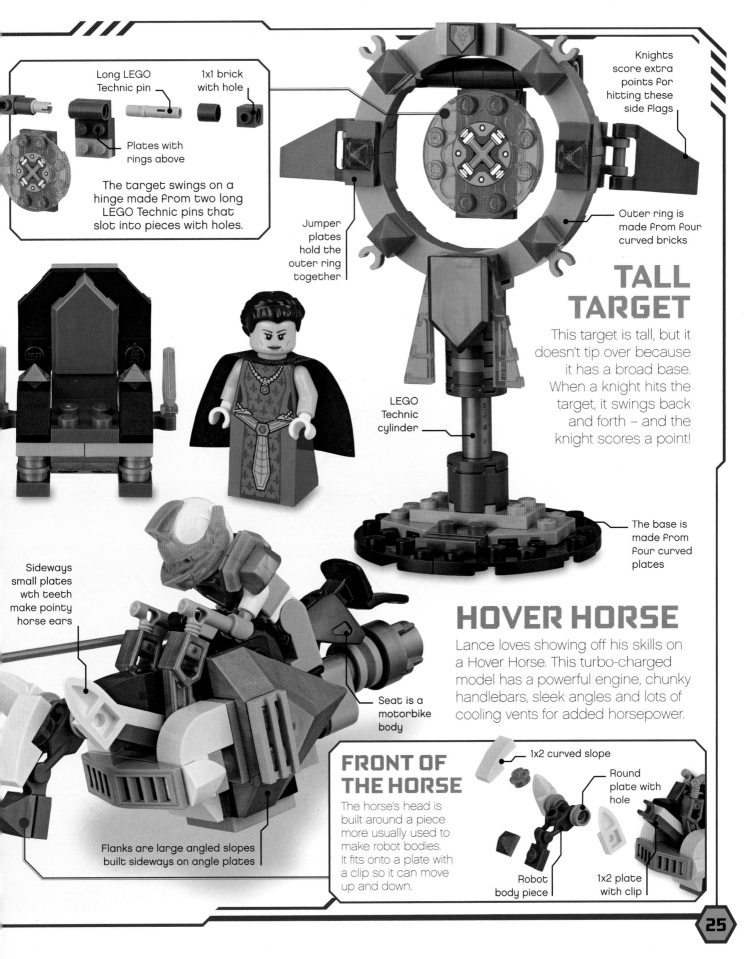

AN UNWELCOME GIFT

King Halbert has so many birthday presents, he needs a whole room to put them in! But one of the gifts is not what it seems… Jestro, the villainous jester, is hiding inside the biggest present. He sneaks out to cause havoc in the king's castle!

SURPRISE! IT'S ME!

PRESENTS

These gifts are all different shapes and sizes. Each one is made mostly from one solid colour to look like wrapping paper. Other colours are added to suggest a ribbon or bow.

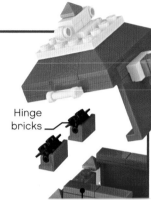

OPENING ACT

This big box opens using a hinge along one side. The other three sides all have smooth tiles where the top part rests on them, so the box opens and closes easily.

Hinge bricks

Smooth tiles

Flower stud

1x1 slope

2x3 plate

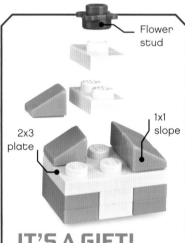

IT'S A GIFT!

Start building this gift in the middle, using a 2x3 white plate that holds all the other pieces together, above and below. A flower stud on top makes a bow to finish.

TIME TO CRASH THIS PARTY.

OPEN VIEW

Plates with side studs make the loops of a bow

Build around the minifigure you want to fit inside

The base is a 6x6 plate

Each side is one wall element

FIREPLACE

The king's castle is full of grand rooms with fancy fixtures, like this fireplace. It has a stone surround, a brass grate and a red tiled hood to carry the smoke away.

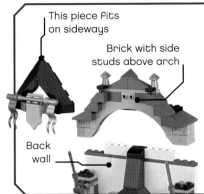

This piece fits on sideways

Brick with side studs above arch

Back wall

BRICK LAYERS

The top of the fireplace has three layers: the back wall, a wide arch and the triangular front section, which fits sideways onto a brick with side studs.

WHAT WILL YOU BUILD?

- Table for a feast
- Birthday cake
- Castle walls

A shield and flags give a real castle feel!

Textured bricks add detail

Transparent bar

Telescope piece

Plate with side clip

1x1 slope

The lanterns are built upside down and clip onto plates with bars.

Slope bricks and a wheel arch make up the fireplace hood

Just three pieces are used to make this small gift

A flame piece stands in the fireplace

DO BOTS GET BIRTHDAYS, TOO?

LIGHTNING STRIKES!

Jestro heads for the tower where the digital wizard Merlok 2.0 keeps watch over Knighton's computer systems. Jestro lets the evil Cloud of Monstrox in through a window, and The Cloud zaps the main server with lightning, making Merlok disappear!

I'LL RAIN SUPREME!

MAIN SERVER

This powerful piece of kit keeps Knighton's computers talking to each other. It is linked to lots of control panels and monitor screens, and needs vents to keep it cool.

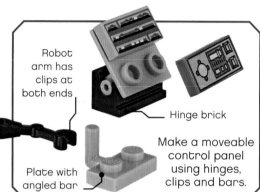

Robot arm has clips at both ends

Hinge brick

Plate with angled bar

Make a moveable control panel using hinges, clips and bars.

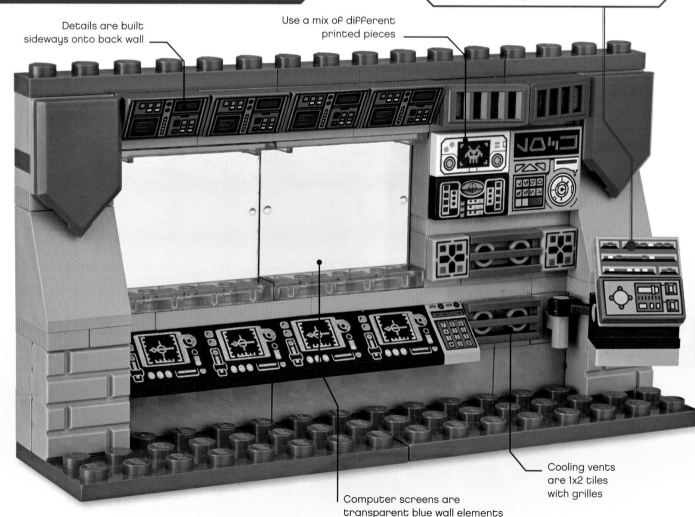

Details are built sideways onto back wall

Use a mix of different printed pieces

Computer screens are transparent blue wall elements

Cooling vents are 1x2 tiles with grilles

MERLOK 2.0

The wizard Merlok lives inside the computer system. This projector allows him to appear in the server room as a hologram. It looks just like an ordinary window when he is not there.

Two inverted half arches make the top of the window

Look out – it's The Cloud!

Holder

Small radar dish

The lamp clips onto the main build using a holder piece.

Each side is one tall column piece

Back section is one castle wall piece

Merlok 2.0 is a special printed piece

HELP!

RIGHT THIS WAY, CLOUD.

AVA'S COMPUTER

Merlok's apprentice, Ava, often uses this station to monitor Knighton's computer network. It has a lamp above it, so she can work into the night. Today, unfortunately, Ava has taken a rare break for the king's birthday!

ROBIN'S PLAN

Computer-whizz Ava realises that something is wrong and rushes to raise the alarm. She explains that all of Knighton's computers have been fried, and fixing them will mean finding four linked servers hidden around the kingdom. Only an expert engineer can do the job – so Robin had better pack his bags!

I CAN FIX THEM!

WELL ARMED

Robin's spinning weapon is built around a four-armed propeller piece and spins on a plate with a pin. A ball-and-socket connection clips it to his Battle Suit.

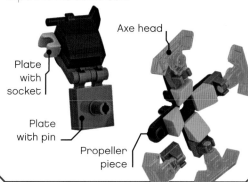

Plate with socket

Axe head

Plate with pin

Propeller piece

Large panel pieces are good for building walls quickly

Sword fits onto plate with clip

Axe heads fit onto plates with top clips

Drawers are sideways jumper plates

MERLOK'S GONE!

WORKSHOP

Robin needs lots of room for inventing things, and his workshop is full of gadgets. His latest creation is an extra left arm for his Battle Suit. The arm is fitted with a mighty spinning wheel of battle-axes.

WHAT WILL YOU BUILD?
- Squire Bot builder
- Stone smasher
- Big screen

Antenna

Radar dish

1x2x2 round brick

2x2x2 round brick

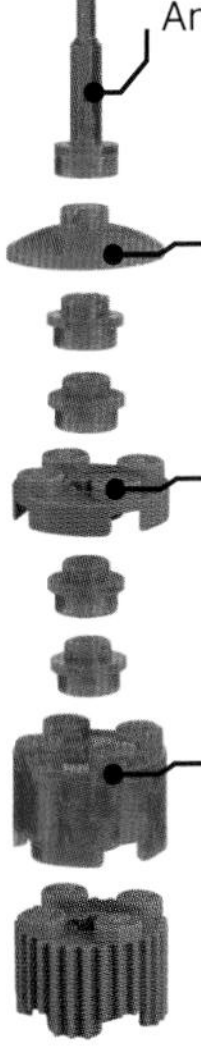

A mix of round parts makes a cool, high-tech aerial.

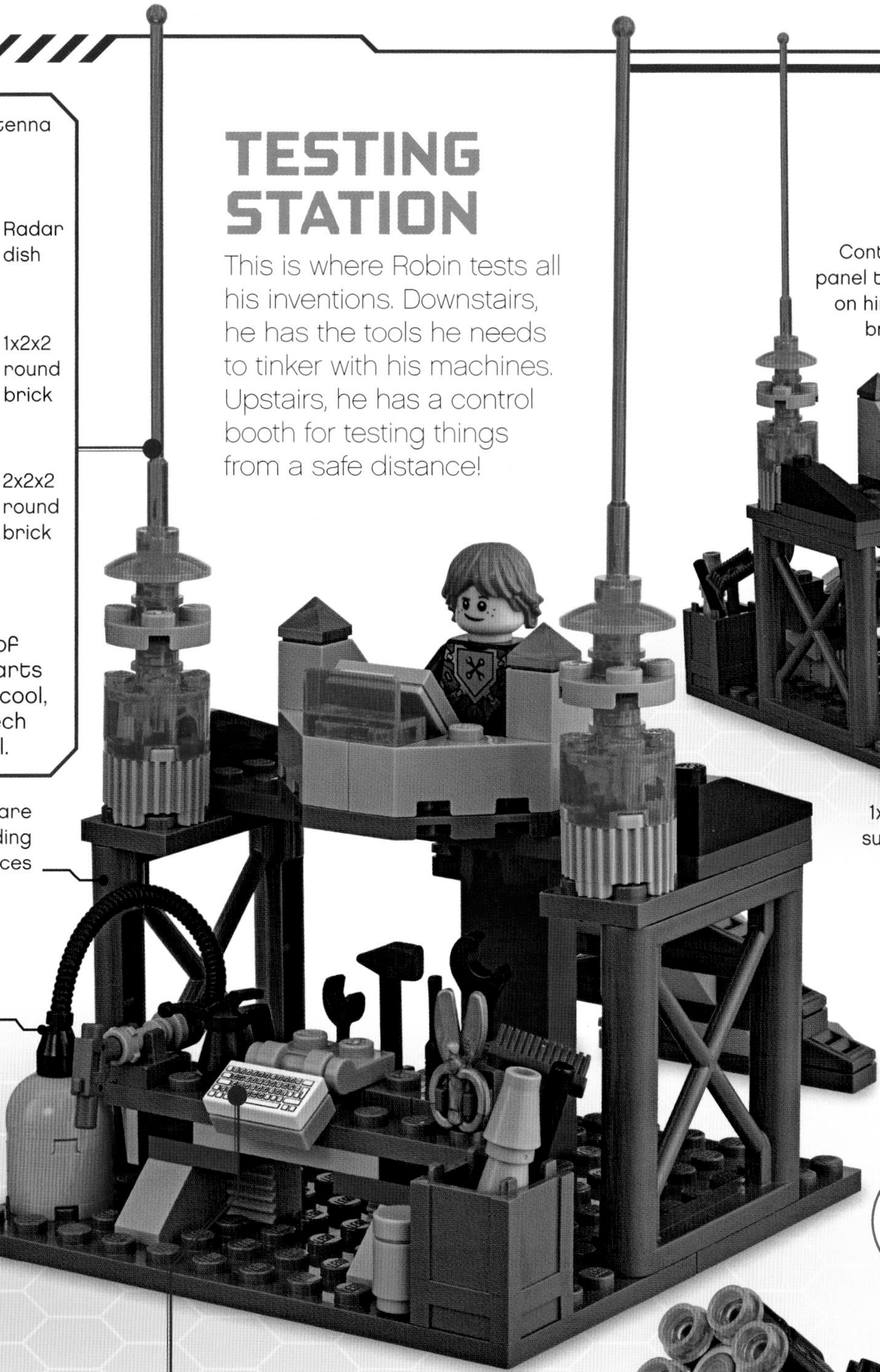

Sides are scaffolding pieces

Hose connects blowtorch to gas canister

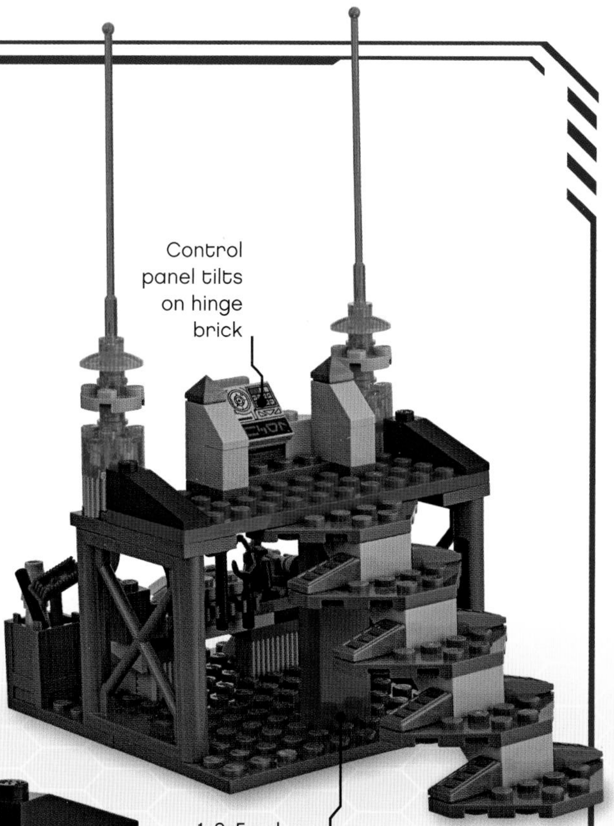

TESTING STATION

This is where Robin tests all his inventions. Downstairs, he has the tools he needs to tinker with his machines. Upstairs, he has a control booth for testing things from a safe distance!

Control panel tilts on hinge brick

1x2x5 column supports the top step

REAR VIEW

I'LL GET THE OTHERS.

Keyboard is a printed tile

ROBIN'S WORKBENCH

Make a realistic-looking workstation by covering it with as many bits of equipment as you can. Robin's bench has spanners, scissors, a keyboard and more – all held on with clips.

Robin's new Battle Suit has passed all its tests!

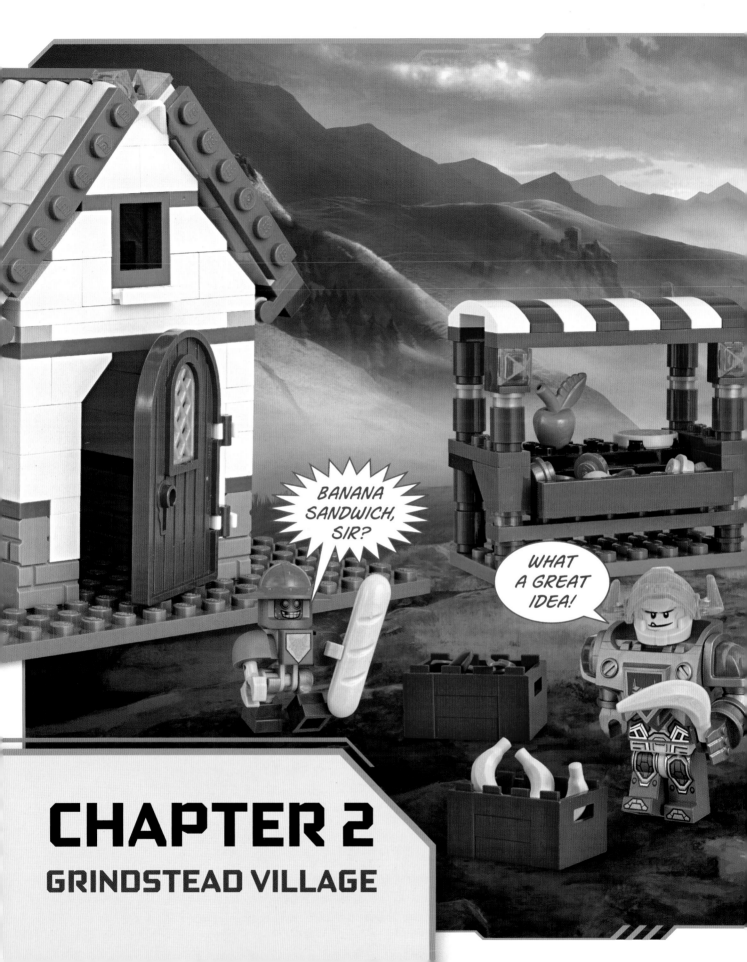

CHAPTER 2
GRINDSTEAD VILLAGE

IT'S GREAT TO BE HOME.

SERVER NO. 1

Robin is very excited to be out on a mission with the knights! Aaron is excited, too, because the first stop on their journey is his hometown: Grindstead Village. The first server is hidden in the village square, in a tall tower surrounded by market stalls. Robin gets out his tools and starts to repair it.

I'M A REAL KNIGHT!

WHAT WILL YOU BUILD?
- Bric-a-brac stall
- Village hall
- Tavern

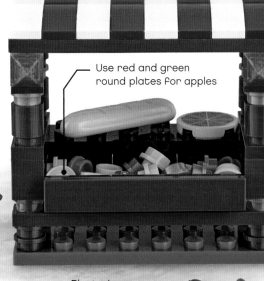

Use red and green round plates for apples

Different-coloured curved slopes make a stripy awning

Brooms and tools fill this box piece

Plant pieces suggest leafy green vegetables

Minifigure sack clips onto the edge of the stall

Grey tiles make a smooth hotplate for cooking

3x4 boxes with handles hold more produce

I SPY A SERVER!

MARKET STALLS

There is lots to buy at Grindstead Village market! These stalls sell a mix of fruit and vegetables, hot food and useful items such as tools and brooms.

CENTRAL TOWER

This grand tower marks the very centre of the village, but its details are not just for decoration. The antenna on top beams information to and from the computer server hidden in its base.

Antenna fits onto a 2x2 radar dish

Mini-shooter missile

Round plate with hole

Bars fit onto plates with clips

These round columns have square bases

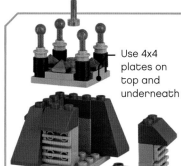

TOP TIPS

Use 4x4 plates on top and underneath

Build the top section separately then add it onto the four columns that make up the sides of the tower. Start with a 4x4 plate, then add tall corner slopes overlapping each corner.

Tall corner slope

SERVER

Robin will be seeing a lot of servers like this one! Spread throughout the kingdom, they all have control panels, cooling vents, and red and green lights to show whether they are working properly.

Plate with handled bar

A handle on the front helps Robin slide the server out of the tower.

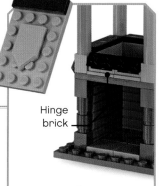

Hinge brick

Use a plate on a pair of hinge bricks to hide the server.

Smooth tiles allow the server to slide in and out

Control panel fits sideways on angle plate

AARON'S COTTAGE

While Robin works, the knights spread out to patrol the streets of the village. Aaron finds himself outside the cottage where he grew up. He can't resist peeking inside his old bedroom – it's here he first dreamed of being a thrill-seeking knight!

LET'S LOOK OUT FOR MONSTERS!

1x2 log brick

1x1 brick with hole

Short LEGO® Technic pin

RAISE A ROOF

Each half of the roof is built separately using log bricks. The blue trim at the sides is made using plates that fit onto short LEGO® Technic pins in bricks with holes.

THE COTTAGE

Aaron's cottage isn't grand, but it is cosy. It is built with a hinged roof so that it's easy to get inside and see what Aaron is up to.

A plate with a rail makes a small window ledge

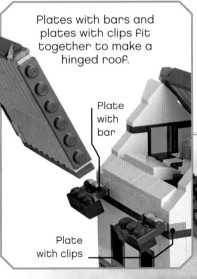

Plates with bars and plates with clips fit together to make a hinged roof.

Plate with bar

Plate with clips

Window pieces are built into the walls

The door swings open on bricks with clips

Fez piece

1x1 nose cone

2x2 round plate

1x1 round plate

You need just six small pieces to make this bedside table and lamp.

A curved slope makes a good pillow

The quilt is made from 16 small tiles

The eaves of the house sit at the ends of a large plate.

A row of smooth slopes tops the side walls

AARON'S ROOM

Aaron's bedroom is squeezed into the roof space of his family home. There is just the right amount of space for Aaron, his bed with its neatly chequered quilt, and his bedside table.

Inverted slopes shape the top of the doorway

Start your build on a plate to keep it stable

I'M A REAL HOMEBOY!

OPEN VIEW

IN AARON'S GARAGE

COOL, RIGHT?

Aaron remembers that he still has some of his old things gathering dust in the garage. His old hover bike may not use the latest technology, but he still loves it – and he can't wait to show it off to the rest of the knights!

GARAGE

The Fox family garage is full of tools for repairing hover tech, plus all sorts of other things that won't fit inside the house. There are old chests and suitcases, books and even a fishing rod.

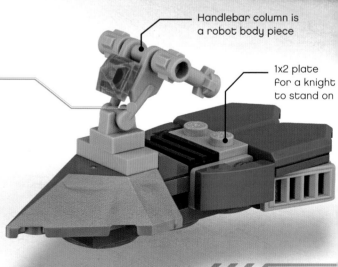

Plates with angled bars make hooks for hanging things

Build an angle plate into the wall to add sideways details

The floor of the garage is two 8x16 plates

HOVER BIKE

Before there were hover shields there were hover bikes. Much bigger than a shield but roughly the same shape, this bit of retro tech has handlebars to hang on to while performing wicked stunts.

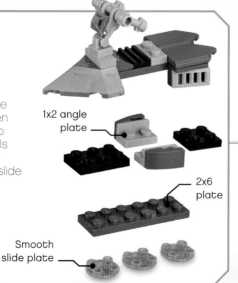

Handlebar column is a robot body piece

1x2 plate for a knight to stand on

HOVER LAYERS

Start your hover bike with a 2x6 plate, then add angle plates so you can build details onto the sides. Use smooth-bottomed slide plates underneath to help your model glide along.

1x2 angle plate

2x6 plate

Smooth slide plate

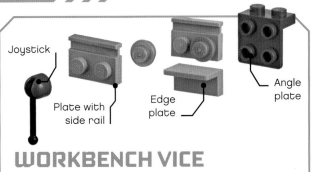

Joystick

Plate with
side rail

Edge
plate

Angle
plate

WORKBENCH VICE

This vice fits onto a workbench built into the garage
wall. It is made from an angle plate and two plates
with side rails, with a joystick piece as the crank.

WHAT WILL YOU BUILD?

- Spare parts rack
- Hover sidecar
- Garage door

A claw slotted into a
brick with a hole makes
this hook for a key

These books are a sideways
stack of 1x2 plates with a
1x2 tile on one end

Four 1x1
plates
with
clips

2x6
plate

SHELF HELP

When building a
wall, add a plate
that is wider than
the bricks around it
to create a shelf.
This shelf also has a
row of clips above it
to make a tool rack.

Be sure to
fill every
corner with
clutter!

*WHO NEEDS
WHEELS?*

AT THE SKATE PARK

LOOK AT AARON GO!

Zipping around on his hover bike, Aaron can't resist trying out a few tricks at the local skate park. This is where he first learned to do awesome stunts. The other knights gather to cheer him on as he shows them some of his favourite moves.

JUMP

This small jump should pose no problem for a record-breaker like Aaron, but it makes for a good warm-up stunt. This one is made using curved slopes, but obstacles like this can be built from anything.

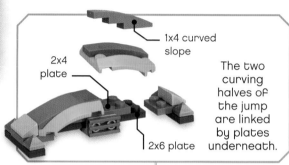

1x4 curved slope

2x4 plate

The two curving halves of the jump are linked by plates underneath.

2x6 plate

These curved parts are more usually used to make the front of vehicles

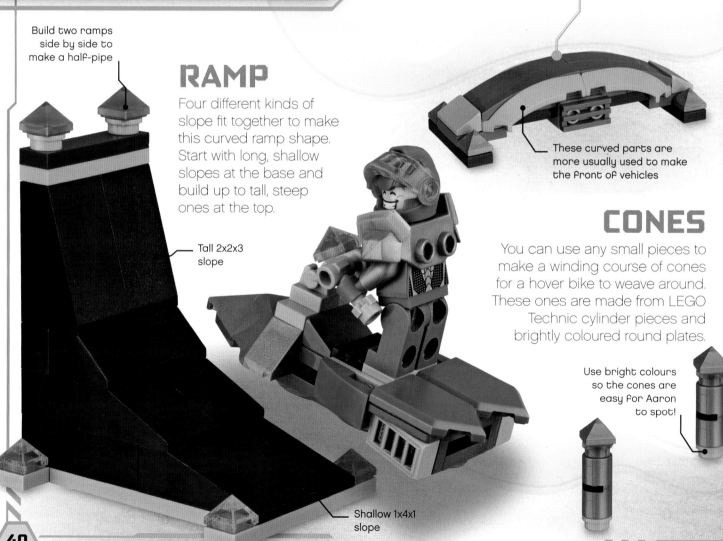

Build two ramps side by side to make a half-pipe

RAMP

Four different kinds of slope fit together to make this curved ramp shape. Start with long, shallow slopes at the base and build up to tall, steep ones at the top.

Tall 2x2x3 slope

CONES

You can use any small pieces to make a winding course of cones for a hover bike to weave around. These ones are made from LEGO Technic cylinder pieces and brightly coloured round plates.

Use bright colours so the cones are easy for Aaron to spot!

Shallow 1x4x1 slope

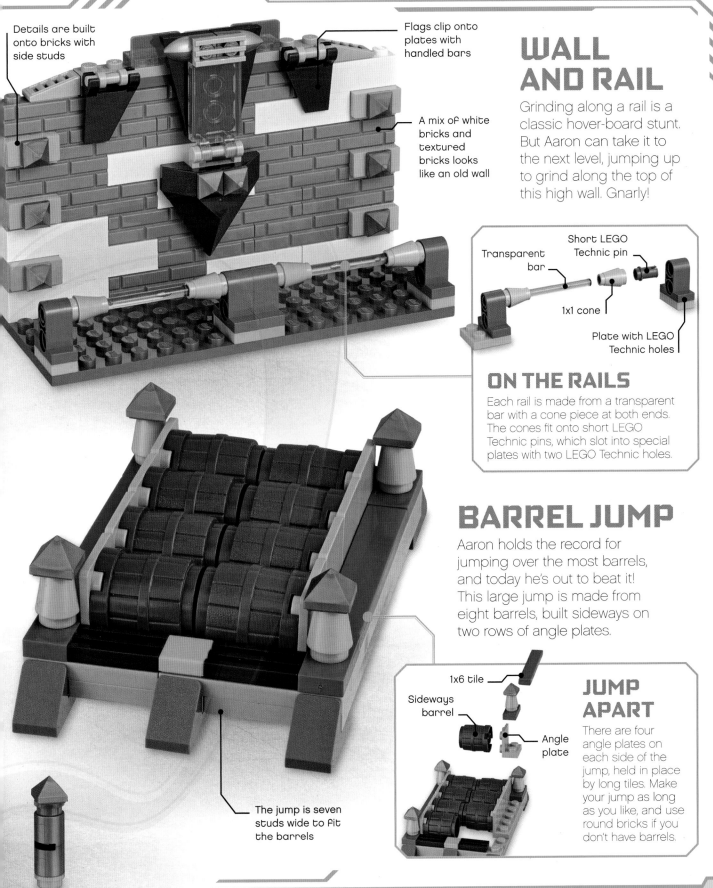

Details are built onto bricks with side studs

Flags clip onto plates with handled bars

A mix of white bricks and textured bricks looks like an old wall

WALL AND RAIL

Grinding along a rail is a classic hover-board stunt. But Aaron can take it to the next level, jumping up to grind along the top of this high wall. Gnarly!

Transparent bar

Short LEGO Technic pin

1x1 cone

Plate with LEGO Technic holes

ON THE RAILS

Each rail is made from a transparent bar with a cone piece at both ends. The cones fit onto short LEGO Technic pins, which slot into special plates with two LEGO Technic holes.

BARREL JUMP

Aaron holds the record for jumping over the most barrels, and today he's out to beat it! This large jump is made from eight barrels, built sideways on two rows of angle plates.

1x6 tile

Sideways barrel

Angle plate

JUMP APART

There are four angle plates on each side of the jump, held in place by long tiles. Make your jump as long as you like, and use round bricks if you don't have barrels.

The jump is seven studs wide to fit the barrels

MONSTER ATTACK!

As Aaron performs a stunt that sends him high into the air, he sees Robin being attacked by Stone Monsters in the village square! The knights rush to fight off the monsters, giving Robin time to grab his Battle Suit and finish his repairs.

TO THE RESCUE!

MONSTER VEHICLE

Stone Monsters are heavy, so they need heavy-duty transport to get around! This beastly battle wagon rolls along on rugged rock wheels and fires lightning bolts from the back.

Round bricks make a cylinder that creates lightning

REAR VIEW

BRING UP THE REAR, AXL!

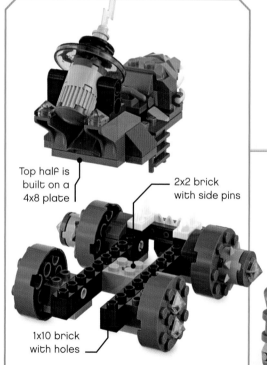

Top half is built on a 4x8 plate

2x2 brick with side pins

1x10 brick with holes

UNDER PINNING
The base of the build is a pair of long bricks with holes, held together by a brick with LEGO Technic style pins on two sides. The top half is built separately.

Lightning bolt slots into round plate with hole

Stack of small radar dishes

Leave space beneath the weapon so it can move

BOLT UPRIGHT

This lightning weapon tilts on a pair of LEGO Technic pins. The pins slot into a round brick with a hole and special plates with two LEGO Technic holes

LEGO Technic friction pin

Special plate with two LEGO Technic holes

2x2 radar dish

Round brick with hole

LET'S ROCK AND ROLL!

Different types of tooth plates make the top and bottom fangs

Entry ladder is a special grille piece

Spiked round bricks keep enemies away!

MONSTER WHEELS

The wheels slot onto the chassis using long LEGO Technic pins.

4x4 round brick

2x2 round tile with centre stud

Brick with hole

Long LEGO Technic pin

WHAT WILL YOU BUILD?

• Monster bike
• Monster garage
• Monster boat

43

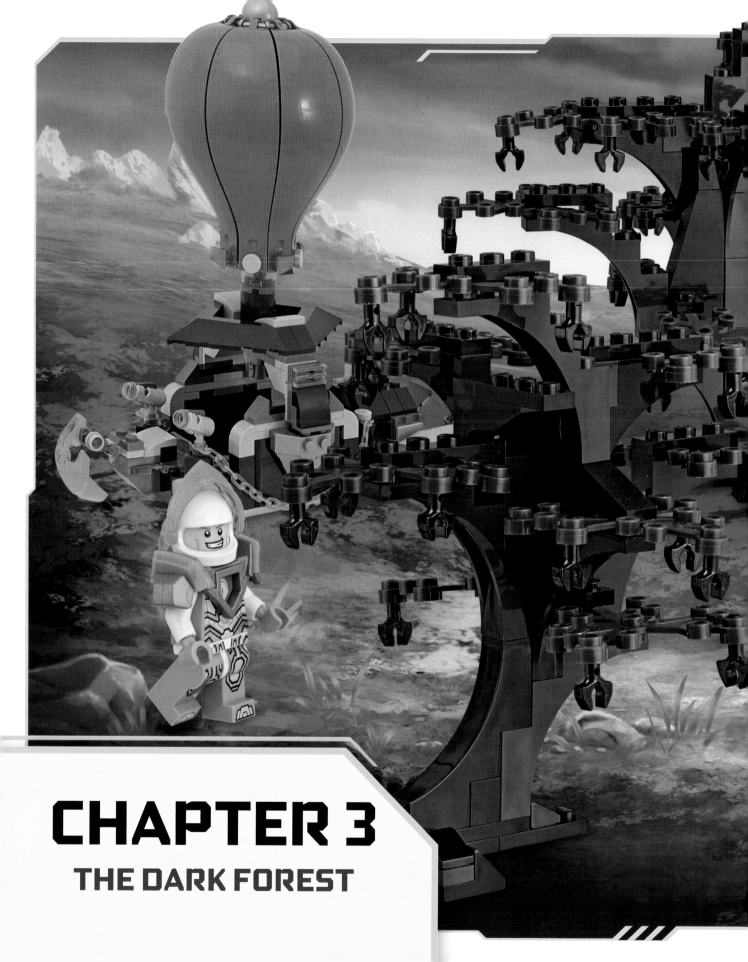

CHAPTER 3
THE DARK FOREST

INTO THE DARK FOREST

The knights' next stop is the spooky Dark Forest. After defeating the Stone Monsters in Grindstead, they know that Monstrox must be on their tail, trying to stop their mission. In an attempt to lose him, the knights set up camp deep in the woods.

ROBINS LIKE TREES!

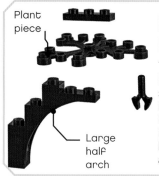

LEAFY BRANCHES

The tree trunk and branches are a mix of slopes, half arches and inverted half arches. Each piece of greenery is sandwiched in place between a half arch and a plate.

Plant piece

Large half arch

TREE

The Dark Forest is full of ancient, spooky-looking trees. Create their jagged branches by slotting claw pieces into the ends of foliage pieces.

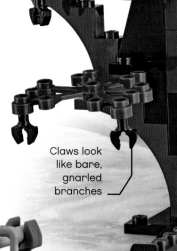

Inverted half arch

Claws look like bare, gnarled branches

Long plates look like roots and keep the tree from tipping over

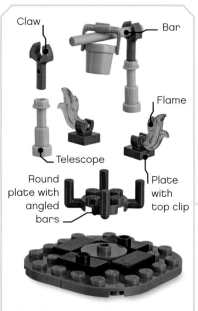

Claw

Bar

Flame

Telescope

Round plate with angled bars

Plate with top clip

BUILD A FIRE

The spit is made from telescope pieces, claw pieces and a bar to hang a bucket from. The flames fit onto plates with top clips, on top of a round plate with angled bars.

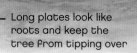

CAMPFIRE

Every campsite needs a campfire. The knights waste no time building a fire with a spit for heating up water and food.

TENT

This big tent has enough room for all the knights. It is held up by tall columns in all four corners and has a colourful canopy on its open side to keep any rain out.

Antenna is 10 studs high

Curved slopes make a smooth top

A crest on the front of the canopy fits onto an angle plate.

Angle plate

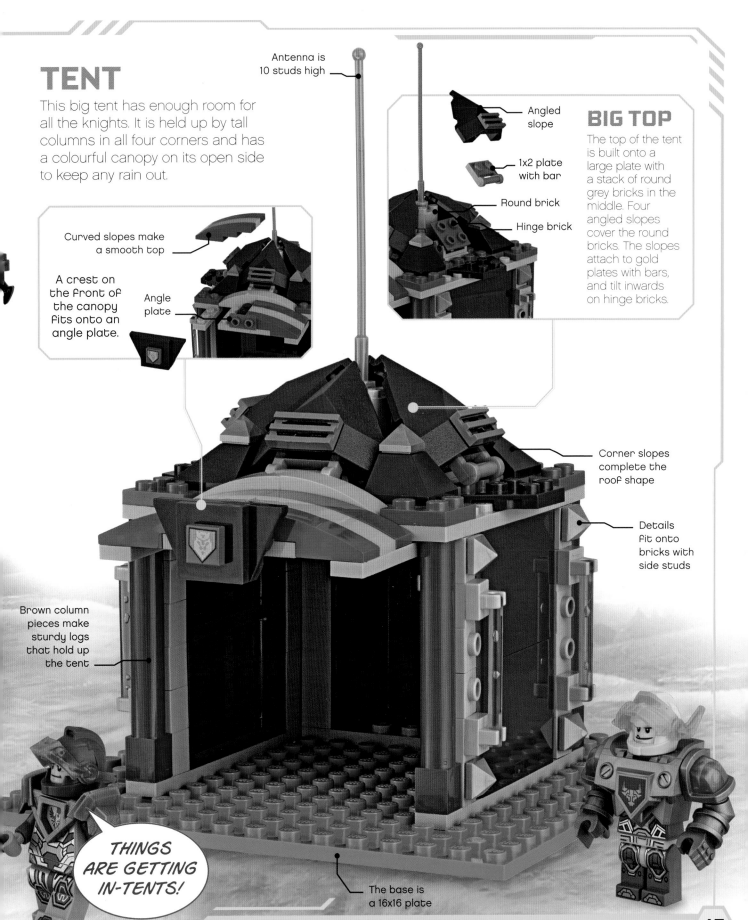

Angled slope

1x2 plate with bar

Round brick

Hinge brick

BIG TOP

The top of the tent is built onto a large plate with a stack of round grey bricks in the middle. Four angled slopes cover the round bricks. The slopes attach to gold plates with bars, and tilt inwards on hinge bricks.

Corner slopes complete the roof shape

Details fit onto bricks with side studs

Brown column pieces make sturdy logs that hold up the tent

THINGS ARE GETTING IN-TENTS!

The base is a 16x16 plate

DANGER BY THE RIVER

Clay grew up near the Dark Forest, so he knows the way through. He leads the knights to a stone bridge that crosses a river. But – oh no! – The Cloud is waiting nearby. He knows that, because the bridge has a face, he can turn it into a Stone Monster.

NONE SHALL PASS!

WHAT'S ON THE OTHER SIDE?

RIVER ROCKS

Over millions of years, rushing river water has carved these rocks into strange, sloping shapes. Make them using a mix of slope bricks and other smooth pieces.

Green slopes look like moss

Log bricks and textured bricks add stonework details

Railings are telescope pieces

WHAT WILL YOU BUILD?

- Drawbridge
- Riverboat
- Jetty

1x12x3 arch

Four of these large arch pieces are used to make the bridge – two at the front and two at the back.

Rocks can be any shape, so let your imagination run wild!

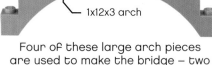

48

STONE BRIDGE

This bridge has lots of details, including a scary face carved into the side! It has three feet supporting two arches to take the knights across the water.

I AM!

The walkway of the bridge is made from long plates that are six studs wide

Monstrox's lightning crackles around the bridge

Fangs are tooth plates

Plate with side clips

Horn

Sloped nose attaches to jumper plate

MONSTER MAKE-UP

Face details are built on sideways. Horn pieces create curved eyebrows above eyes made of yellow round plates centred on jumper plates.

A base of blue suggests the surrounding water

Add some plant pieces growing among the rocks

Smooth round tiles make pebbles and stepping stones

MONSTER CHASE

A flash of lightning turns the bridge into a trio of Stone Monsters – right beneath the poor knights' feet! With no Merlok to grant them NEXO Powers, the knights work together to roll boulders towards the monsters. This forces the monsters into the river, where they are safely washed away!

TIME TO ROCK AND ROLL!

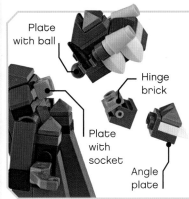

STONY FACED

Each monster's neck is a ball-and-socket joint, so its head can turn in any direction. A hinge brick allows the fanged mouth to hang open and snap closed.

Plate with ball

Hinge brick

Plate with socket

Angle plate

Eyes are cones on plates with side rings

RAWR!

Sideways slopes add shape to back

Upper fangs are four 1x1 tooth plates

Claw hand slots onto plate with angled bar

BRIDGE MONSTERS

These stone-cold stompers have moveable legs for chasing after their enemies! They also have big, biting mouths and rotating claw hands. The knights had better move fast!

BOULDERS

The boulders in this part of the forest have blue precious metals running through them. Their real value, however, comes when the knights roll them towards the bridge monsters!

Slopes make jagged rock edges

Peaked slope

Steep, double height slope

Standard slope brick

Inverted slope

ROCK BREAKING

Rocks can be any shape or size, so you can use any bricks to make them! Different-sized slopes and inverted slopes work especially well, turned in all directions.

THIS BRIDGE HAS CROSSED US!

Horns fit onto plates with side clips

Arms are sideways curved slopes

Lower fangs are a 1x2 tooth plate

Using pre-built rock parts as well as your own small builds is a quick way to expand a rocky landscape.

FOREST FIND

NOW WE'RE REALLY FLYING!

As soon as they are safely on the other side of the river, the knights spot an old airship that has been left to rust in the forest. With the help of his trusty tools, Robin manages to get it working again and they take off. The knights can now search for the next server from high above the treetops.

FRONT VIEW

AIRSHIP

This high-tech airship looks like a complicated build, but it is actually a fairly simple box shape with smaller builds for the front, back and top added on at the end.

CLEARED FOR TAKE OFF!

Octagonal ring adds detail to engines

Stud shooters fit into the ends of chain pieces

The airship is eight studs across – wide enough even for Axl!

WHAT WILL YOU BUILD?

- Battle Suit glider
- Stone catapult
- Helicopter

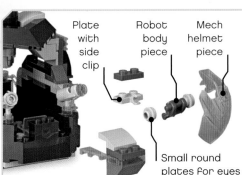

Plate with side clip

Robot body piece

Mech helmet piece

Small round plates for eyes

FIGUREHEAD

Like a giant Hover Horse, the airship has an impressive adjustable head at the front. It is made from four pieces and attaches to a plate with a side clip in the front of the airship.

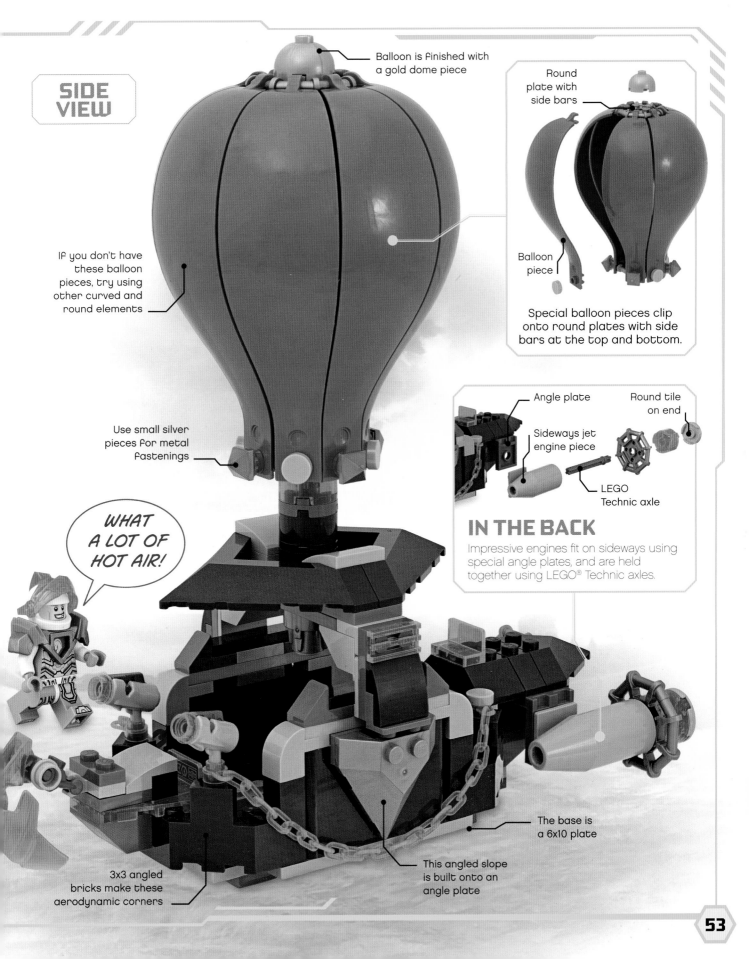

Balloon is finished with a gold dome piece

Round plate with side bars

If you don't have these balloon pieces, try using other curved and round elements

Balloon piece

Special balloon pieces clip onto round plates with side bars at the top and bottom.

Angle plate

Round tile on end

Sideways jet engine piece

Use small silver pieces for metal fastenings

LEGO Technic axle

IN THE BACK

Impressive engines fit on sideways using special angle plates, and are held together using LEGO® Technic axles.

WHAT A LOT OF HOT AIR!

3x3 angled bricks make these aerodynamic corners

This angled slope is built onto an angle plate

The base is a 6x10 plate

SERVER NO. 2

From high up in the airship, the knights quickly spot the tree house where the second server is hidden. They tether the airship to a nearby tree and descend down on ropes. The knights explore the forest while Robin fixes the server. They will be back in the air in no time at all!

THIS ROBIN CAN FLY!

RAISE A ROOF

2x3 tile with side clips

Bar

1x1 slopes hold roof in position

Hinge brick

The roof is made from tiles with side clips, held together with a bar. Each side of the roof is fixed in place on two hinge bricks.

Add a small shooter missile on each end

TREE HOUSE

This treetop cabin is built on the base of a once-mighty oak. The hollow trunk makes a great hiding place, while the sentry box above is a perfect lookout point.

LOOK – A GUARD FROG!

Log bricks look like chopped wood

Tall column is one large piece

Orange foliage suggests autumn is coming

A mix of slopes makes a realistic trunk and roots

FRONT VIEW

MOVING STAIRCASE

To make it easy to access the server, the stairs swing upwards on a hinge. The moveable parts are made from LEGO Technic pins and 1x1 bricks with holes.

Staircase is all one piece

1x1 brick with hole

WHAT WILL YOU BUILD?

- Forest cabin
- Treetop walkway
- Monster trap

UNDER THE STAIRS

The server fits in the 4x4 space inside the tree house. Line the floor of this section with smooth tiles so the server can slide in and out easily.

Side is a single brown rock piece

Round bricks make a tree stump

A small radar dish and a cone make a realistic toadstool

A smooth tile stops the stairs from fixing onto the base

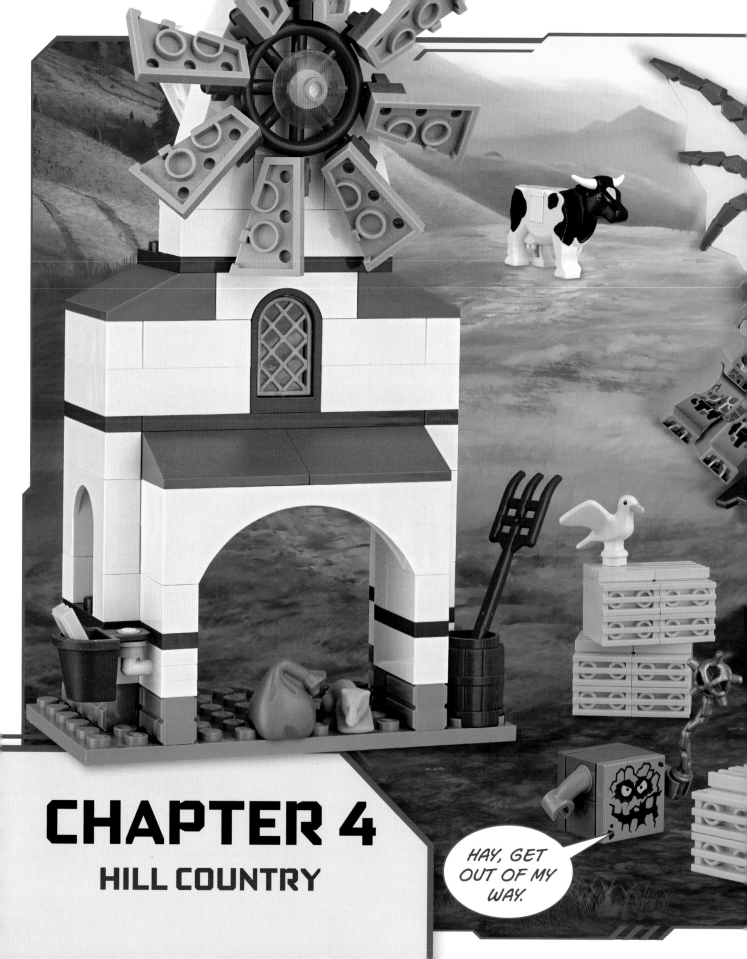

CHAPTER 4
HILL COUNTRY

THE STOLEN SERVER

Welcome to Hill Country! Axl knows where the server is hidden, so the knights leave the airship and stroll into town, even finding time to eat on the way. But when they get to the windmill where the server should be, there is only an empty space!

I SMELL LUNCH!

SPIT ROAST

This outdoor kitchen is a bigger version of the campfire the knights made in the forest. It has a handle to turn the spit so the food gets cooked evenly.

Propeller piece

LEGO® Technic axle

Plate with angled bar

LEGO Technic connector with round hole

TURNING TIPS

The spit is a LEGO Technic axle suspended between two LEGO Technic connectors on plates with angled bars. Food pieces can be attached to a propeller piece slotted onto the axle.

STEAK STICK

Axl's steaks are attached to three plates with clips that fit onto a 1x1 brick with two side studs. A cone piece connects this brick to a bar piece, which slots into the rotating spit.

Bar piece

Cone piece

1x1 brick with two side studs

This fish is clipped onto a smaller side grill

Turning this crank rotates the spit

Three steaks can be cooked at the same time

2x1 slope

Logs are cone pieces attached to crank

Plates with clips hold the food in place

Red, orange and yellow transparent pieces look like glowing hot coals

AXL DOESN'T NEED A SERVER!

58

Radar dish connected by stud to ship's wheel

Ship's wheel piece

The sails are angled plates fitted onto a ship's wheel using plates with top clips.

FANTAIL

Wheel piece connects to brick with round hole

Brick with a cross hole

This fantail is made with a 2x2 plate with wings, two jumper plates, two clips, a flag piece, and a bar piece. The bar piece slots into a brick with a cross hole.

1x4 arch brick over window

WINDMILL

This mill tower uses a handful of slopes and arches to make a tall, distinctive shape. It has moving sails and a large space where the missing server should be.

Basket holds hay for farm animals

1x8x2 arch brick

Angled roof

Crank piece

Full sack of flour

OH WELL, WE'LL LOOK ELSEWHERE.

WELL

This well is where the Hill Country townsfolk get their water. It has a handle for lowering and raising water buckets, and a roof to keep out falling leaves.

Hinge plates

ON THE FARM

Axl grew up (and up!) in Hill Country, so he knows his way around. When Macy spots Stone Monster footprints, Axl realises the monsters have taken the server to an old stone fort. He leads his friends to a farm so they can borrow a vehicle – then they drive off in search of the crumbly crooks!

FOLLOW THOSE FOOTPRINTS!

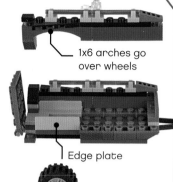

ON THE TRAIL

The trailer has edge plates running inside the wheel arches so its cargo can't get caught up in the wheels. Edge plates are slimmer than bricks, so leave more space inside the trailer.

1x6 arches go over wheels

Edge plate

TRAILER

This trailer has room to store plenty of hay bales – or plenty of knights! To make it the right height, build the tractor first, then design the trailer alongside it.

The tailgate is a 4x4 plate with clips linked by a bar to a 1x2 plate with clips.

1x2 plate with clips

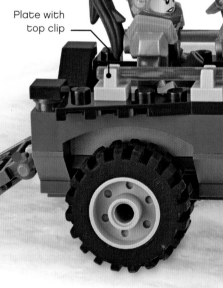

Plate with top clip

Inverted slopes make the trailer wider at the top than the bottom

GET A MOOOOVE ON!

HAY BALES

This hay has been harvested by the farmer and gathered into bales for feeding her cattle. That's if the birds don't eat it all first, of course!

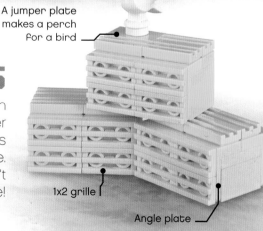

A jumper plate makes a perch for a bird

1x2 grille

Angle plate

COW FIELD

The farmer keeps her cows in a field with high-tech fences around the edges. If a cow tries to cross a fence, it sets off an alarm and the farmer comes running!

Bars and bricks with clips make the fence posts

The tap is a claw on a telescope

This cattle trough is the perfect height for the cow to drink from

Transparent tiles and round bricks make the main fence

IN THE DRIVING SEAT

The tractor's cab has space for a driver in chunky armour. The front of the cab is made up of angled plates with an angled transparent red windscreen on top.

Edge plates make space for the driver's arms

Windscreen

Angled plate

HOLD ON, KNIGHTS!

Front grille and bumper are built sideways on angle plates

The base of the tractor is two 1x12 bricks with holes

1x2 drawbar plate with ball

1x4 plate with socket

A ball-and-socket joint connects the trailer to the tractor.

TRACTOR

This powerful tractor has big wheels with plenty of grip for going up and down rocky, muddy hills. It's perfect for chasing through Hill Country in search of the missing server.

WHAT WILL YOU BUILD?
• Tractor shed
• High-tech gate
• Barn

FIGHT FOR THE FORT

It isn't long before the knights spot the old fort in the distance, but before they can reach it, they have to get past the defences. Stone Monsters have taken over a scary watchtower – and are patrolling the area in a huge monster guardian.

LOOK OUT – A LOOKOUT!

MONSTER GUARDIAN

This big-armed brute is out to grab anyone who comes near. It is controlled by a Stone Monster who sits inside, and can turn in any direction thanks to a turntable piece.

SCARY ARMS

The guardian's arms swivel on balls built into LEGO Technic angle beams. The same angle beams secure the top of the head, which slots onto LEGO Technic pins.

Long LEGO Technic pin with axle end

Sideways plate with ring

LEGO Technic pin with ball joint

Angle beam

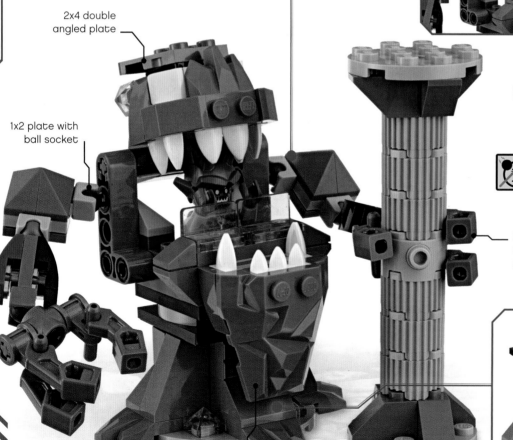

2x4 double angled plate

1x2 plate with ball socket

I HATE STONE ARMIES!

Moveable fingers can grab knights

4x4 round plate

4x4 turntable

The guardian twists on a 4x4 turntable halfway up its body.

Front is a sideways rocky piece

WATCHTOWER

This watchtower has three carved faces, and Monstrox could turn it into a terrifying Stone Monster at any moment! Only the bravest knight would dare approach.

Two blades with LEGO Technic holes make striking eyes and eyebrows

This step allows the guards to see over the walls

The ladder can be raised to keep out intruders

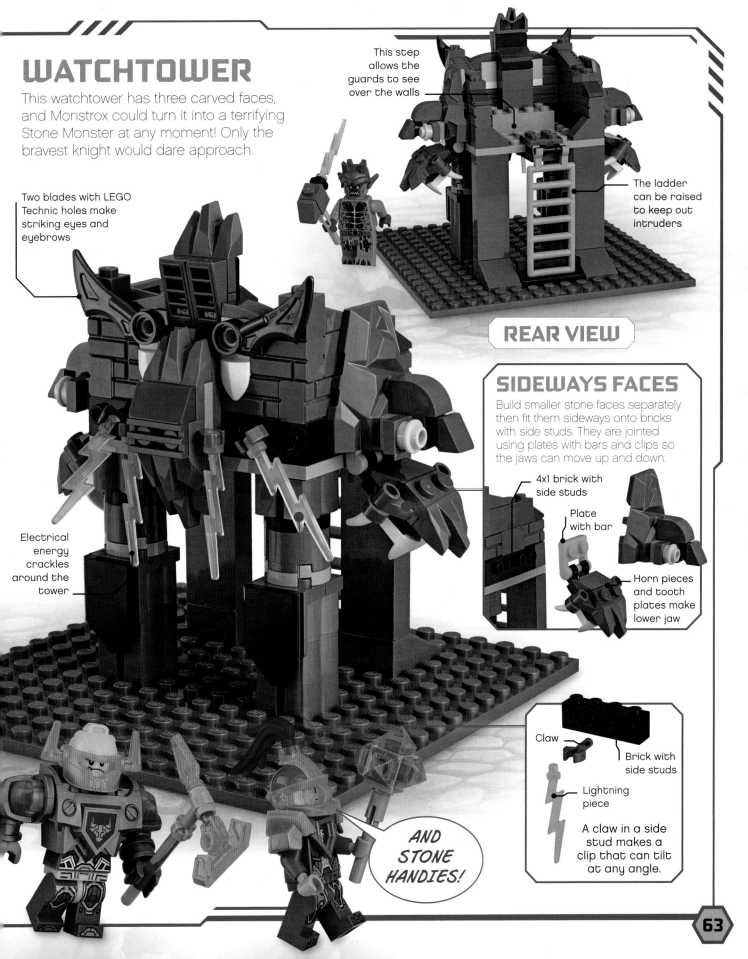

REAR VIEW

SIDEWAYS FACES

Build smaller stone faces separately then fit them sideways onto bricks with side studs. They are jointed using plates with bars and clips so the jaws can move up and down.

4x1 brick with side studs

Plate with bar

Horn pieces and tooth plates make lower jaw

Electrical energy crackles around the tower

Claw

Brick with side studs

Lightning piece

A claw in a side stud makes a clip that can tilt at any angle.

AND STONE HANDIES!

SERVER NO. 3

The knights fight their way past the Stone Monsters and arrive at the fort – where they find even more Stone Monsters! Robin puts on his Battle Suit and climbs over the walls to grab the server, while the other knights stand guard. They escape and put the server back in its place.

I'M GOING IN!

WHAT WILL YOU BUILD?

- Battering ram
- Fort prison
- Catapult

STONE FORT

This old stone fort has started to crumble over the years, making its walls jagged and uneven. But its fierce stone face is still intact and buzzing with Monstrox's lightning energy!

Hinge plate

HANDY HINGES

Hinge plates link three separate builds to make one long, angled wall. Building a pair of hinge plates into each join, rather than just one, makes for a stronger connection.

The two sides of the fort are similar but not the same

A mix of slope bricks makes interesting rocky shapes

Transparent blue tiles suggest a water-filled moat

SERVER REAR VIEW

The server is hidden behind the wall

These monstrous nostrils are short LEGO Technic pins in bricks with holes

Fence pieces create barred windows in the walls

I'VE HEARD OF WALLS WITH EARS, BUT...

A STONY GLARE

The staring stone eyes are built sideways on an angle plate with each eyeball centred on a jumper plate. The eyelids are wheel arch pieces, with curved slopes for eyebrows.

Curved slope

Wheel arch

Angle plate

Jumper plate

Ball with hole

Different kinds of tooth plates make the top and bottom teeth

1x4 brick with 4 side studs

Rocky slopes linked by plates fit sideways onto bricks with side studs.

2x4 plate

2x2 plate

EVIL TRANSPORT DETECTED.

CHAPTER 5
AUREMVILLE

SERVER NO. 4

The final broken server is hidden behind a high wall in the glitzy town of Auremville. This is where Lance grew up, surrounded by gold streets and marble buildings. Robin doesn't have time to see the sights, though. He has to finish repairing Knighton's computer system!

THREE DOWN, ONE TO GO!

AUREMVILLE STREET

The streets of Auremville are literally paved with gold! Beside them, gleaming white columns and high-security walls keep sightseers out of private property – but this wall isn't all it seems!

1x4 arches link the tops of the columns

Each column is a stack of 2x2 round bricks

Neat picket fences mark out public gardens

Different-coloured smooth tiles make paving slabs and cobbles

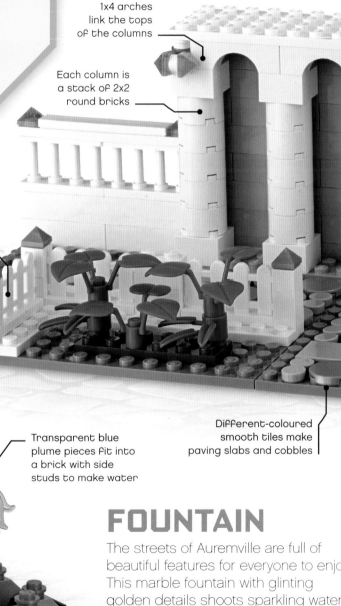

Upside-down round plate with hole

This upside-down antenna slots into the pieces below

Upside-down brick with four side studs

Upside-down small cone

Upside-down medium radar dish

2x2 round plate

2x2 grooved round brick

An aerial connects upside-down elements to upright ones to make the fountain.

Transparent blue flame piece

Upside-down small radar dish

Transparent blue plume pieces fit into a brick with side studs to make water

FOUNTAIN

The streets of Auremville are full of beautiful features for everyone to enjoy. This marble fountain with glinting golden details shoots sparkling water into the air, then down into a pool.

The base is four large corner plates in a cross shape

SECRET ENTRANCE

This brick wall is actually a door in disguise! It has hinge plates at the top and bottom that connect it to one of the grey columns, so it can swing open.

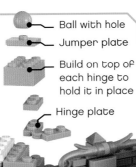

- Ball with hole
- Jumper plate
- Build on top of each hinge to hold it in place
- Hinge plate

WHAT WILL YOU BUILD?

- Marble sculpture
- Street crossing
- Street signs

SHADOWPLAY

The archways are built with solid grey walls behind them. This helps them stand out and creates the illusion of a shadowy space behind.

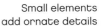

- Large white plate covers the grey on top
- 1x4 arch
- Small elements add ornate details

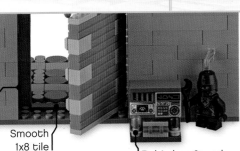

Smooth 1x8 tile

The back of this wall is one stud narrower than the front

REAR VIEW

Robin has found the final server!

BEHIND THE DOOR

The closed door rests on a smooth tile to slide open easily. The back wall is slightly narrower on the opening side so the door doesn't get stuck.

GOOD LUCK, ROBIN!

RICHMOND MANSION

As Robin gets to work fixing the server, Lance takes the other knights to see his family mansion, where generations of Richmonds have lived in style. They pass grand gates – and even a security Bot – on the way to see Lance's car collection.

COME ON IN!

SENTRY BOX

A security Bot guards the gate to Lance's mansion. It spends all day standing to attention in this sentry box. The box has a security camera and a keypad for opening the main gate.

Camera is a small engine piece

Sideways plate with top clip

Lens is a transparent round piece

This simple security camera clips onto a plate with an angled bar.

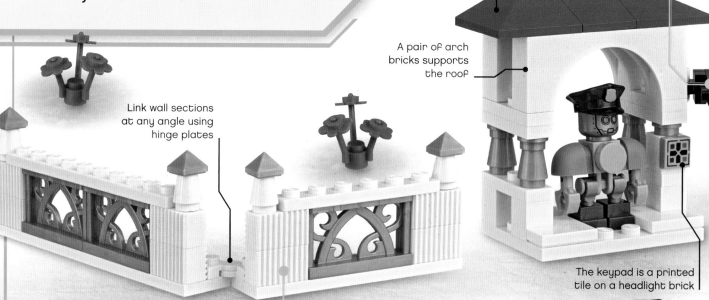

3x3 corner slope

A pair of arch bricks supports the roof

Link wall sections at any angle using hinge plates

The keypad is a printed tile on a headlight brick

LOOK OF LUXURY

Each section of wall has textured bricks at the ends and one or two fancy fence pieces in the middle. The walls are widest at the bottom so they don't tip over.

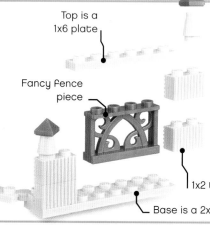

Top is a 1x6 plate

Fancy fence piece

1x2 textured brick

Base is a 2x8 plate

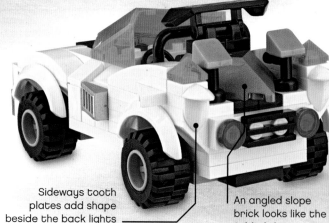

Sideways tooth plates add shape beside the back lights

An angled slope brick looks like the folded-down roof

REAR VIEW

ENTRY GATE

Grand golden gates welcome Lance and his friends to the Richmond mansion. A huge arch sweeps over the gates, linking two tall columns, both of which have security cameras on top.

A mix of slopes and inverted slopes make up the roof

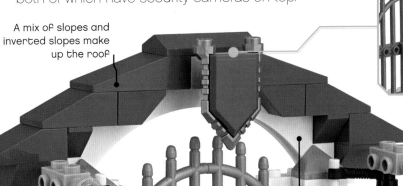

CLIPPED ON

1x2 brick with side clip

Brick with two side clips

Each gate fits onto a 1x1x3 brick with two side clips, which make a much stronger connection than a single clip. The shield above the gate fits onto a 1x2 brick with side clip.

MARBLE WALLS

The Richmond family likes to have guests, but only if they're invited. For that reason, they have gold and marble walls all around their estate. Some of their visitors come along just to see the walls!

Two large half arches make the top of the gateway

This handle is a nozzle piece

The spoiler fits onto two 1x1 plates with top clips

The windscreen fits onto a jumper plate at the front

This gold bumper is two sideways curved bows

SPORTS CAR

This speedy soft-top is the pride of Lance's car collection. It has chunky wheels and a big, powerful body, but still manages to look sleek and stylish. Its engine is 600 Hover-Horsepower!

Smooth slopes and curves add realism by covering all the studs

A WORLD OF WHEELS

It's not only sports cars in Lance's collection. He also has quad bikes and a golf buggy! The knights use the vehicles to patrol Auremville's streets. Suddenly, they hear the roar of a mighty engine, and the sound of a laughing jester!

SHH! THAT SOUNDS LIKE...

WHAT WILL YOU BUILD?

- Stretch limo
- Vintage car
- Drag racer

UTILITY QUAD

This quad bike is built for strength not speed, and can cover even the toughest terrain with ease. It has handlebars like a bike, but four wheels like a car.

I LOVE THE SCREECH OF TYRES!

REAR VIEW

Both quad bikes have a clip on the back to hold a weapon or a shield.

Brick with side clip

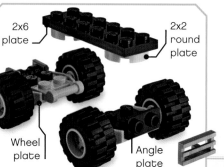

2x6 plate

2x2 round plate

Wheel plate

Angle plate at front

SANDWICH PLATES

The build begins with a 2x6 plate. The wheel plates go underneath, with elements for fitting details onto the front and back sandwiched in between.

The headlights are smooth round tiles

Even Axl can fit in this wide vehicle!

This grille fits onto an angle plate

The curved roof pieces fit onto this 2x4 plate

Slim edge and corner panels add room to this storage compartment

The cab lifts open on two plates with top clips

REAR VIEW

This front section is all one piece

GOLF BUGGY

A golf buggy might not be standard transport for a knight, but this little off-roader is silent and speedy. It has space for storing weapons and a wraparound cab for protection.

Shield clips onto back

I THOUGHT THAT WAS YOUR SINGING.

A transparent edge piece makes a small windscreen

WHEEL LOCK

The tyres of this quad are chunky enough that the base can be built underneath the wheel plates. This locks the wheel plates securely in place once the top section is built on.

Front section overlaps back

2x6 slope plate

SPEED QUAD

This four-wheeler is smaller than the utility quad, but much quicker. Its base is built close to the ground so it stays stable as Macy zips through the streets of Auremville.

JESTRO COMES TO TOWN

Watch out – it's Jestro! He is driving into town in a monster truck, and The Cloud isn't far behind. The knights race after him in Lance's fleet of cars. They must get to Robin before Jestro and The Cloud can stop him from fixing the final server.

YOU CAN'T CATCH ME!

MONSTER TRUCK

This monster truck really lives up to its name, with glaring eyes and lightning bolts pointing at anyone who gets in its way. Its raised back section also makes it look like it is ready to pounce.

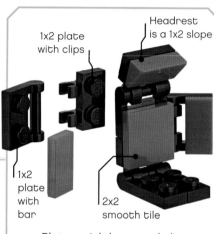

1x2 plate with clips

Headrest is a 1x2 slope

1x2 plate with bar

2x2 smooth tile

Plates with bars and clips fit with tiles to make a smooth, adjustable seat.

The round tiles on the wheels fit onto LEGO® Technic half pins

Yellow eyes add to the monster look

Rear spoiler piece used as a front mudguard

A hook and winch can be used to help the truck over tricky terrain

I'M RIGHT BEHIND YOU, JESTRO!

SO ARE WE!

Plates with end tubes make cooling vents for the engine

Front wheels fit onto special plates with LEGO Technic holes

This socket plate can be used to pull a trailer

LEGO Technic pins connect LEGO Technic cylinders

REAR VIEW

Brick with hole

LEGO Technic pin

Angle beam

Back axle

Long LEGO Technic pin

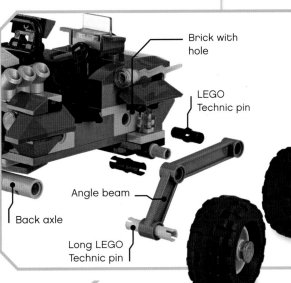

A DIFFERENT AXLE

The truck has bricks with holes on both sides, connected to angle beams using LEGO Technic pins. For added strength, longer LEGO Technic pins connect the back wheels and the back axle.

WHAT WILL YOU BUILD?

- Monster road bike
- Monster jet
- Road block

ROBIN RULES!

The knights reach Robin just in time to see him taking on a Stone Monster in his Battle Suit! Jestro is too late. Robin has fixed the last server, bringing back power to all the computers in Knighton – and Merlok! Robin blasts the monster with his six-stud shooter, and the knights chase Jestro out of town!

I'M BACK!

STONE MONSTER

This massive monster is the biggest foe Robin has ever battled! Its huge clawed hands can move in all directions, and its powerful legs and feet make it hard to knock down!

Each shoulder is made with click hinge connections

A single rocky piece makes three jagged claws

Sideways curved slopes add bulk to the body

Plate with side ring

Round plate with pin

This monster helmet has holes on the sides to build out from.

AN IDEA WITH LEGS

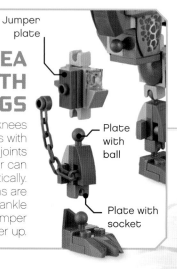

Jumper plate

Plate with ball

Plate with socket

Build the hips, knees and ankles with ball-and-socket joints so the monster can move realistically. Clanking chains are built in at the ankle and fit onto jumper plates higher up.

Big feet stop the monster from tipping over

Lightning fires from the monster's helmet

2x3 angled plate

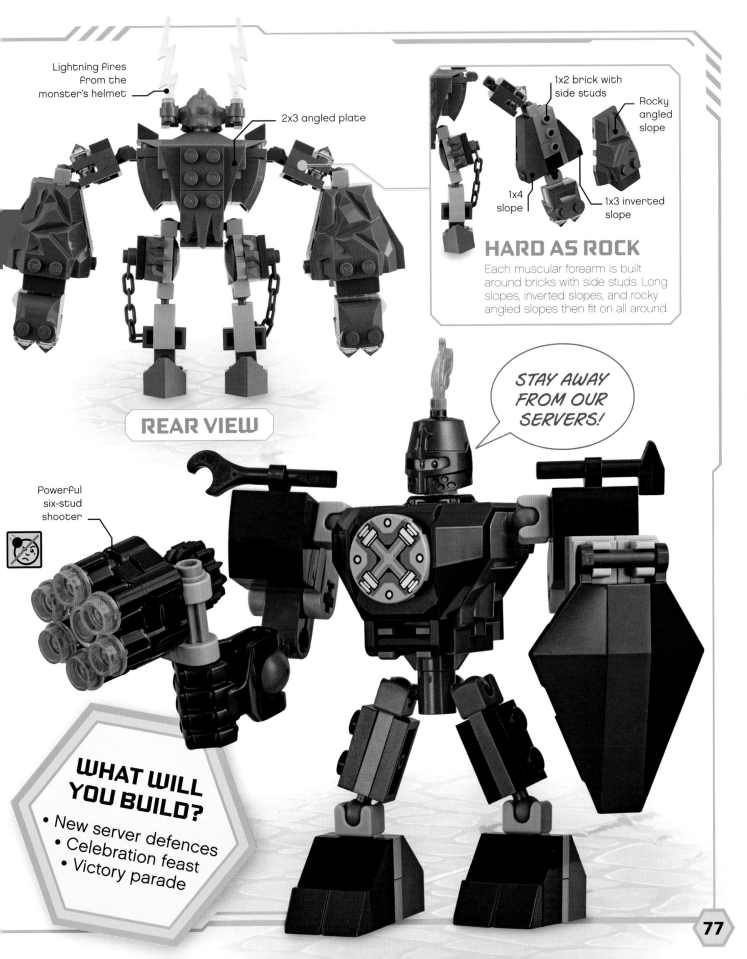

1x2 brick with side studs

Rocky angled slope

1x4 slope

1x3 inverted slope

HARD AS ROCK

Each muscular forearm is built around bricks with side studs. Long slopes, inverted slopes, and rocky angled slopes then fit on all around.

REAR VIEW

STAY AWAY FROM OUR SERVERS!

Powerful six-stud shooter

WHAT WILL YOU BUILD?

- New server defences
- Celebration feast
- Victory parade

THANK YOU, ROBIN!

With Knighton safe once again, the knights and Robin gather at Knighton Castle, where Merlok 2.0 is waiting. King and Queen Halbert have organized a party to celebrate Knighton's newest hero. Robin is excited to have helped the knights, but can't wait to get back to his workshop. His next project will be to build defences for all the servers so that Jestro can't break them again!

Penguin
Random
House

Senior Editor Laura Palosuo
Editorial Coordinator Clare Millar
Project Art Editor Jenny Edwards
Senior Designers David McDonald,
Mark Penfound
Pre-Production Producer Siu Yin Chan
Producer Louise Daly
Managing Editor Paula Regan
Managing Art Editor Jo Connor
Design Manager Guy Harvey
Creative Manager Sarah Harland
Art Director Lisa Lanzarini
Publisher Julie Ferris
Publishing Director Simon Beecroft

Written by Simon Hugo
Inspirational models built by Jason Briscoe
Photography by Gary Ombler
Additional design by Gary Hyde

Dorling Kindersley would like to thank
Randi Sørensen, Heidi K. Jensen, Paul Hansford,
Martin Leighton Lindhardt, Raphaël Pretesacque,
Mikkel Lee, Susan Due, Michael Vibede Vanting
and Charlotte Neidhardt at the LEGO Group.

First published in Great Britain in 2017 by
Dorling Kindersley Limited, 80 Strand, London WC2R 0RL
A Penguin Random House Company

004–298786–July/17

Page design copyright © 2017 Dorling Kindersley Limited.

LEGO, the LEGO logo, the Brick and Knob configurations, the
Minifigure, NEXO KNIGHTS and the NEXO KNIGHTS logo are
trademarks of the LEGO Group. © 2017 The LEGO Group.
Manufactured by Dorling Kindersley under licence
from the LEGO Group.

A CIP catalogue record for this book
is available from the British Library.

ISBN: 978-0-2413-1978-9

Printed and bound in China

www.LEGO.com
www.dk.com

A WORLD OF IDEAS:
SEE ALL THERE IS TO KNOW

I'M STILL WAITING FOR DINNER!